Mexican Coat
of Arms in
Santa Anna's Day

FOREBODING START

FEBRUARY 21, 1794: George Washington struggles through an agonizing second term as President of the United States. France is gripped by the Reign of Terror. Blood runs in the gutters of Paris. In Mexico, Santa Anna is born.

It was a disturbed, brutal world into which Antonio Lopez de Santa Anna emerged. And his personality reflected it. Paradoxically, the name Santa Anna means SAINT ANNE, mother of the Virgin Mary!

Antonio was of Spanish descent. He had almost no formal education and was described as a quarrelsome schoolboy. When grown to manhood he bragged that he had read only one book!

His father, a mortgage broker, wanted Antonio to become a businessman. But the strong-willed youngster would have none of it. For him the only life was·that of a soldier. When he was just 16 he lied about his age to get into the

Spanish army as a cadet. At that time Mexico was a Spanish colony.

Antonio joined the cavalry and began to hero-worship his commander, a ferocious wretch named Arredondo. This man's influence on the boy during Antonio's formative years reinforced the worst traits in Santa Anna's character.

By the age 19 Antonio was a first lieutenant. The year was 1813. General Arredondo received orders to cross the Rio Grande and put down the first rebellion for freedom by the inhabitants of Texas. The rebels were a badly trained mob of Mexicans, Americans and Indians. In no sense were they a match for the crack Spanish regiment. Arredondo butchered them. It was young Antonio's first taste of battle, and he got a citation for bravery! Arredondo's savage methods deeply impressed him. Right then and there two fatal illusions took root in the boy's mind: (1) Texans must be handled harshly and (2) Texans can't fight!

STAINED REPUTATION

IT WAS DURING this campaign that Santa Anna made his first trip to San Antonio, which even then was the center of rebel resistance. Arredondo mercilessly subdued the place, captured the Alamo, and ordered mass murders and executions. Then he turned his troops loose upon the townspeople to pillage, torture and rape. Finally the soldiers were exhausted. Santa Anna, an inveterate gambler, sought relaxation at the gaming tables. In no time at all he was arrested for forging Arredondo's and another senior officer's signatures on checks. The regimental surgeon, Jaime Garza generously lent the young lieutenant

SANTA ANNA
ON THE BATTLEFIELD

300 pesos to help him out. But Antonio's personal belongings, even his sabre, were confiscated. Much of his property was sold to satisfy the debt. Even so, less than half the obligation was ever paid off. And Antonio steadfastly refused to reimburse Dr. Garza. The scandal of the forgeries was covered up for a time. But in later years it slithered into the light repeatedly to embarrass Santa Anna.

By 1821 the 27-year old Antonio was a captain in the royal Spanish army. But revolutionary feeling against Spanish domination was mushrooming in Mexico. All at once there appeared a brilliant swashbuckler to spearhead the revolt. His name was Augustin Iturbide. Ostensibly patriotic, he was like Santa Anna, an opportunist. But he knew how to sway the populace. Mexicans flocked to his standard. And revolution engulfed the land.

SWIFT SWITCH

THE REBELS called for Santa Anna's support. In reply Antonio led his royalist troops against them in a morning battle. Some insurgents were killed, many more captured. Santa Anna won the engagement. At two o'clock that afternoon, strong rebel reinforcements rushed onto the field. Now an unbelievable thing happened. Antonio deserted the royalists and went over to the other side! This was but the first in a long series of about-faces for Santa Anna. He was to demonstrate again and again his ability to betray causes and friends whenever it would benefit him personally.

That same day the Spanish viceroy, on hearing of Santa Anna's morning defeat of the rebels and unaware that the victor had defected, sent him a promotion to lieutenant colonel. Learning of this, Antonio, who had earlier been promised a promotion by the insurgents if he would desert the royalists, demanded and got the rank of full colonel in the rebel army. Two promotions in a single day!

Iturbide won his revolution and had himself crowned Emperor of Mexico! He made Santa Anna a brigadier general. "I will be your loyal subject and defender until death," Antonio wrote the emperor. In less than 6 months the young brigadier would be plotting to dethrone Iturbide. Meanwhile, attempting to get closer to the emperor's warm side, 28-year old Antonio proposed marriage to Iturbide's 60-year old sister. The emperor rejected the idea with a sneer.

EMPEROR'S SUSPICIONS

ITURBIDE'S TARNISHED CHARACTER was similar to Santa Anna's. Both men were conceited, unprincipled and ruthless but had great personal magnetism. The emperor became suspicious and jealous of his ambitious young brigadier who was growing alarmingly powerful. So Iturbide arranged to subtly strip Antonio of much of his authority. Santa Anna, no fool, knew what was going on. He also realized that, Mexican politics being what they were, his life was probably in danger. Antonio moved fast. He denounced Iturbide and bellowed in favor of a republic. Afterward, speaking to a friend, he confided that when he yelled for a republic he had not the slightest idea what a republic was! In openly rebelling against his emperor he could easily have gotten himself shot. Many times later in his chaotic career Santa Anna brushed even closer to death. But on each occasion he survived. A guardian devil — in his case it couldn't have been an angel! — must have protected him.

Incredibly, Antonio's outburst against Iturbide precipitated a chain of events that knocked the emperor off his throne and drove him into exile!

"HERO OF TAMPICO"

THE FIRST MEXICAN REPUBLIC was established. And a national flag and coat of arms were designed. The flag, a tricolor of green, white and red, symbolized independence (green), the purity of the Catholic faith (white) and

Spanish and Mexican elements united (red). The eagle and snake coat of arms memorialized the famous Eagle and Serpent of Aztec mythology. By tradition, the Aztecs had settled near the present site of Mexico City when they encountered an eagle rending a serpent.

In 1829 the Spanish tried to reconquer Mexico. An invading force under General Isidro Barradas set sail for Tampico. But 200 Spaniards were lost during storms in the Gulf of Mexico. On reaching Tampico more of Barradas' men were felled by yellow fever. Meanwhile Santa Anna, efficiently organizing an army, set out to oppose the Spaniards. When the Mexican troops got to Tampico they didn't have much trouble subduing the weakened invaders. Barradas surrendered and sailed away.

As might be expected, Santa Anna milked every drop of glory possible from the incident. "Savior of the Country" the Mexicans called him. Overnight he became a national hero. His mediocre victory over the Spanish elevated him to an almost mythological status. Forever after he was to be known as "The Hero of Tampico". Mexican President Guerrero named him a full general.

ELECTED PRESIDENT

POSING as a Federalist, Santa Anna won the presidency of Mexico in 1833. He was 39. In the Mexico of that day a Federalist was one who believed in decentralized government, no privileged classes and equal rights for all. Santa Anna was never really a Federalist. After winning the election he made an incredible request. He asked permission to retire to his extensive country holdings, to rest from the fatigues of military campaigning. He would leave

SANTA ANNA ENJOYS HIS FIGHTING COCKS

his vice president, Gomez Farias to act as chief executive! Santa Anna's wish was granted. He had enjoyed the scheming and skullduggery employed to capture the presidency. It did wonders for his overblown vanity to win the highest post in the land. But administering the office he knew would bore him. So he just sat back, took things easy and amused himself with his fighting cocks. All the while he watched closely every move the vice president made. Farias was a genuine Federalist, compassionate and extremely able. So long as people approved of the vice president's actions, Santa Anna took full credit for them. But when one day the fickle public turned against Farias,

Santa Anna came roaring out of retirement protesting that the vice president had not "consulted" him! He dashed to Mexico City, ran Farias out of office, took power into his own hands — and did another about-face! Dropping all pretense of Federalism, he assumed the role of dictator. Sadly, Mexico, with its selfish special classes and abysmally ignorant masses, was not ready for an enlightened government like Gomez Farias honestly tried to give it.

TEXANS ON RAMPAGE

NOW, during Santa Anna's first presidency, bad news came from Texas. The troublesome ruffians in that northern province were revolting again! "Well, small matter", thought Santa Anna. After all had he not learned under Arredondo, nearly a quarter-century before, how to deal with sloppily trained, no-good Texans? This time he'd punish them so severely they'd never even think revolution again! His brother-in-law, General Cos was sent up to Texas to do the job. The Texans whaled the daylight out of Cos and his army. After extracting from the general his word of honor that he and his troops would never again take up arms against them, the Texans benevolently freed them and sent them packing back to Mexico!

When news of Cos' defeat reached Santa Anna that proud, vainglorious Mexican turned black with rage. Those cursed Texans! Humiliate him would they! He, godlike Master of all Mexico, would take to the field himself. Now the Texas rabble would be beaten into the earth!

VENGEANCE

WITH ENERGY born of a furious urge for revenge, Santa Anna whipped together a force of 8,000 men. Not many regulars could be spared — they had been decimated by recurring revolutions and counterrevolutions in Mexico. The multitude was called the Mexican army, but not all Mexicans were in favor of it. A lot of the troops were foreigners — European and American adventurers. The most deadly sniper was an Illinois man named Johnson!

In mid-winter Santa Anna pushed his armed host toward Texas. The frigid, wind-battered deserts of northern Mexico took their toll. Men and animals died by the hundreds. At the Rio Grande, Cos' brigade met the expedition. Santa Anna demanded that his brother-in-law break his oath to the Texans and lead his troops against them again. Cos obeyed. A hundred miles from San Antonio General Sesma's brigade joined them. Overwhelming might was marching against the Alamo.

Sam Houston, Texas commander, had ordered the men in the Alamo to evacuate that fort and withdraw. But they responded that they "had rather die in these ditches than give them up to the enemy."

On the afternoon of February 23, 1836 Santa Anna, astride a saddle sumptuously plated with gold, rode into San Antonio. A $7,000 sabre glittered at his side. Imperiously, His Excellency ordered a blood-red banner run up atop San Fernando Cathedral, serving notice to the Alamo's hapless defenders that they would be given no quarter.

Only 182 men held the Alamo against Santa Anna's horde of thousands. But it took the Mexicans almost two weeks to conquer the tiny garrison. Not until March 6, in the midst of a bonechilling Texas norther, did the Alamo fall. Santa Anna had no part in the final battle. He supervised it from more than a quarter of a mile away, surrounded by all his regimental bands blaring forth throughout the action. Inside the mission itself, in the darkness and smoke of the last assault, the maddened Mexican troops, unable to tell friend from foe, stabbed and bayonetted each other!

FEARFUL COST

WHEN IT WAS all over, Santa Anna airily dismissed the Alamo conquest as "a small affair". Actually he had lost 1,544 of his best men. 500 more were wounded. Mexican Colonel Alamonte commented, "Another such victory will ruin us."

As many of the Mexican dead as possible were given the rites of the Church and buried. Texan corpses were contemptuously stacked like cord wood and burned. All but one, that is. The single exception was the body of a Mexican defender of the Alamo. Santa Anna had compassion for the 12-year old brother of the Mexican rebel. His Excellency asked the sobbing boy to point out his brother's corpse. Santa Anna then directed that it be given Christian burial. This illustrates another facet of the Mexican dictator's twisted character: he could be magnanimous on occasion.

All women and children and a slave boy within the Alamo were spared. Among these was Mrs. Susanna Dickinson and her baby daughter Angelina. Santa Anna was so captivated by tiny Angelina that he urged her mother to let him adopt the child. Mrs. Dickinson of course refused.

UNFAITHFUL

AT THIS TIME Santa Anna had for 12 years been married to an admirable woman, Inez Garcia, who was highly respected by all who knew her. But His Excellency was a lecher. During the siege of the Alamo he had thoroughly enjoyed himself in San Antonio. One of his generals, Castrillon by name, innocently described to the President an exquisite, well-bred 17-year old girl he had seen in town that day. Santa Anna, knowing Castrillon's superb taste, told him to bring the girl to him pronto. Castrillon indignantly refused, protesting that being a procurer was not in line of military duty. The President quickly found another officer more obliging. Santa Anna met the lovely girl, courted her, proposed marriage and was accepted. A very solemn, very bogus wedding ceremony was then performed by a soldier masquerading as a priest!

Three weeks after the Alamo fell Santa Anna permitted the massacre of James W. Fannin and 389 other men at Goliad. Six weeks following the Alamo battle the Mexican dictator's own wounded veterans were still languishing in San Antonio, suffering horribly from lack of medical attention, with lead bullets yet in their bodies.

SAM HOUSTON

ON APRIL 21 the armies of Santa Anna and Sam Houston collided at San Jacinto. In a battle lasting only 18 minutes the Mexican forces were routed. His Excellency disguised himself in a private soldier's uniform and tried to sneak away. But he was captured and dragged before Houston. Texans on all sides clamored for the Mexican president's immediate death. Santa Anna visibly quaked with fear. Strange how this man, at times recklessly brave, could occasionally be a miserable coward. Santa Anna was a drug addict. His courage probably came out of the opium bottle. Certainly in this instance it did. He begged for his opium supply which had been siezed. It was handed him. Dosing himself, he became calm and immediately started bargaining with Houston! Meanwhile the Texas commander had loudly silenced those who demanded Santa Anna's execution. Houston well knew that the Mexican was worth more to the Texas cause alive than dead.

Santa Anna tried to flatter the Texas leader by complimenting him on capturing "The Napoleon of the West," as His Excellency modestly referred to himself. Houston, unimpressed, dealt firmly with him and forced the Mexican president to agree to a peace treaty.

When Santa Anna's camp equipment was brought into Texan headquarters, it was found to include silver teapots and cream pitchers, monogrammed china, cut glass tumblers, cut glass decanters with gold stoppers, a silk tent, silk sheets, silk underwear and a set of $1,700 diamond studs!

The Mexican dictator realized that Houston had saved his life. Forever after he admired the Texas leader. One of the strangest episodes in history is the cordial correspondence carried on between the two after Houston became President of the Texas Republic. These protagonists in the Texas Revolution were a lot alike in some ways. They were born within a year of each other. Houston

SAM HOUSTON

was the older. Both were slated for business careers but rejected the idea. Each was sensitive, complex, inconsistent and an egoist. Each loved to "ham it up", to dramatize himself. They were innate leaders of men, natural politicians, masterful military organizers and had strong appeal for women. But whereas Houston, with all his human weaknesses, was one of nature's true noblemen, Santa Anna was a monstrous scoundrel with scarcely a shred of decency.

ROUGH TREATMENT

THE MEXICAN PRESIDENT was held in Texas while Houston went to New Orleans to undergo treatment for a severe leg wound received at San Jacinto. During Houston's absence Santa Anna signed a treaty in which he swore never again to take up arms against Texas and agreed that hostilities between Mexico and Texas should cease at once. In the meantime he was subjected to much indignity, kept on a ball and chain for 53 days, at times not even fed, and very nearly lynched. When Houston got back to Texas Santa Anna was so glad to see him he literally sobbed on the Texas commander's big shoulder!

A vote taken throughout Texas showed that sentiment was overwhelmingly in favor of Texas joining the U.S.A. as a state. But there was much opposition to this in America. Sam Houston, just elected President of the Texas Republic, and Stephen F. Austin decided to send Santa Anna to Washington, D.C. to talk to President Andrew Jackson about the matter. The Mexican dictator had come up with a plan whereby the U.S. could buy Texas from Mexico. In January, 1837 Santa Anna spent six fruitless days talking to Jackson in Washington. The U.S. president was aware that Santa Anna had been repudiated by Mexico since his imprisonment in Texas. Jackson assured the Mexican that the U.S. would consider buying Texas only if the offer came through regular diplomatic channels. Then Santa Anna was permitted to sail back home.

In Mexico he found himself completely discredited and even suspected of treason. He gave the populace one of his bombastic addresses assuring them of his loyalty and declaring his determination to retire to private life forever. His "retirement" didn't last 18 months!

PASTRY WAR

THE FRENCH blockaded the important Mexican port of

SANTA ANNA ESCAPES IN HIS UNDERWEAR

Vera Cruz in 1838, to force payment of claims on behalf of French nationals. These claims had been outstanding for 10 years. The most notable demand was one submitted by a French pastry chef whose bakery had been pillaged by Mexican soldiers in 1828. So the armed conflict between Mexicans and French in 1838 became known as the "Pastry War".

Here was the chance to redeem himself that Santa Anna had been waiting for! He volunteered to lead troops against the French, and was permitted to do so. Pompously arriving in Vera Cruz, he handled things so badly that at 5 o'clock one morning he narrowly escaped being captured by French troops. He ran from the enemy wearing nothing but his underwear! Later in the day, however, he reappeared splendidly uniformed astride a white charger, prancing at the head of an insignificant column of troops. Defiantly he rode down to the harbor where French vessels were anchored. A ship's cannon belched fire. The General's horse was killed beneath him. He himself received a grievous wound below the left knee and his lower leg had to be amputated.

Santa Anna lost a limb but retrieved his lost reputation! Now that he had given his leg for his country, he was once again the nation's idol. Of small importance that the Mexicans did not win the "Pastry War", that French claims were paid as demanded — though at a reduced rate thanks to the influence of the British government.

For the second time we see Santa Anna back in the Mexican president's chair! Altogether he served 5 times as president and 5 times was kicked out of Mexico into exile!

EYEWITNESS

FANNY CALDERON DE LA BARCA had been reared in the U.S. and became the wife of Spain's first Minister to independent Mexico. She possessed penetrating feminine insight. In 1839 she visited Santa Anna and his charming wife at their hacienda while the General was in temporary retirement. Here in part is her personal description of the Mexican leader who incidentally was a man 5 feet 10 inches tall: ". . . a gentlemanly, rather melancholy-looking person, decidedly the best-looking and most interesting figure in the group. He has a sallow complexion, fine dark eyes, soft and penetrating and an interesting expression of face. Knowing nothing of his past history one would have said a philosopher, living in dignified retirement — one who had tried the world and found that all was vanity, one who had suffered ingratitude and who, if he were ever persuaded to emerge from his retreat, would only do so to benefit his country. It is strange how frequently this expression of philosophic resignation, of placid sadness, is to be remarked on the countenances of the most cunning, most ambitious, most designing and most dangerous statesmen I have seen. They have a something that would persuade the multitude that they are above the world, and engage in its toils only to benefit others — so that one can hardly persuade oneself that these men are not saints. Above all, witness the melancholy and philosophic Santa Anna.

"He was quiet and gentlemanly in his manners, perhaps one of the worst men in the world — ambitious of power — greedy of money — and unprincipled — having feathered his nest at the expense of the republic — and waiting in a dignified retreat only till the moment comes for putting himself at the head of another revolution."

HOLY LEG

DURING HIS THIRD TERM as president, Santa Anna, true to character, broke his solemn vow to never again take up arms against Texas. In 1842 he sent General Adrian Woll to raid San Antonio. Fortunately the expedition accomplished little. That same year the leg Santa Anna lost at Vera Cruz, having been disinterred, was carried in a crystal urn in the midst of a huge procession through the streets of Mexico City to the Santa Paula cemetery. There, with great ceremony, in the presence of His Excellency, it was reverently placed inside an ornate gilded monument. Future generations of Mexican citizens, especially young military officers, were supposed to be inspired by the enshrined limb.

Late in the summer of 1844 Santa Anna's wife, Inez Garcia died. It was a blow. For despite his infidelity, he loved and respected this good woman. But he did not grieve too long. In little more than a month the 50-year old widower married beautiful young Dolores de Tosta, aged 15.

Mexicans had highly esteemed Santa Anna's first wife. The president's failure to observe a respectable mourning period for her angered them. By the end of 1844 Santa Anna's callous attitude and tyrannical methods had turned the tide against him. He was driven from office. His sacred leg was hauled from its monument and trailed through the streets. His statues were pulled down. Realizing the hopelessness of the situation he offered to "resign" the presidency and go into exile "for the only and noble" purpose of averting civil war. One of his stipulations, however, was that his statues should be restored! He was scorned. Knowing there was no time to lose, he disguised himself and fled.

SPOOKY INTERLUDE

SANTA ANNA OWNED tremendous acreage in his native state of Vera Cruz. But he had always been heartily disliked there. Early one evening, on the last lap of his flight, he found himself in a forest nine miles south of Jalapa, his home town. Suddenly he was fired upon and surrounded by Indians. These none-too-civilized redskins had already heard that Santa Anna, hated owner of all the surrounding country, was trying to escape from Mexico. Noting that their captive had a wooden leg, the Indians interrogated

Dolores, Santa Anna's 15-Year Old Bride

him. Quickly they realized that they indeed had the tyrant.

Now occurred something eerie. Instead of holding Santa Anna for a reward these barbarians hit upon an idea as innovative as it was grisly. They lugged forth a huge earthenware cauldron, sent into the forest for quantities of a particular kind of banana leaf, and brought great handfuls of chiles and peppers from their huts. Their plan was to boil the despised landowner alive. Then correctly spiced, his body would be wrapped in banana leaves and handed over to the authorities as a gigantic tamale. The Indians thought the government officials who wanted so much to get hold of Santa Anna would enjoy such a practical joke! At this point the local priest happened on the scene. He sprinted to the church and started tugging at the bell rope.

Bong! Clang! Bong! This clamor could inevitably be depended upon to cool Indians' overheated spirits. Next he grabbed the holy vessel containing the Host. With this in hand he rushed toward the Indians commanding them to spare their victim. The childlike savages could not defy the holy man. Sullenly they acquiesced.

Santa Anna was turned over to the authorities and jailed in the gloomy fortress of Perote where in the past he had locked up so many Texans. After being imprisoned for nearly 6 months, on June 3, 1845 he was sent into exile for the first time — supposedly for life!

WAR WITH U.S.

IN LITTLE MORE than a year Santa Anna was back in Mexico! He had tricked U.S. President Polk into helping him return on the pretext that he could end the war then going on between the U.S. and Mexico. Once on Mexican soil, Santa Anna soon regained the presidency! He assumed personal command of the army in the field and with marked bravery fought General Taylor at Buena Vista. The battle was a draw, but Mexican losses were 1,500 men to America's 750. Now Santa Anna swung south to face General Scott at Cerro Gordo. Stubbornly refusing to accept sensible suggestions from his subordinates, the Mexican was defeated.

He began to negotiate with Scott. The American general gave him $10,000 to soften up Mexicans who resisted a negotiated peace. Santa Anna proposed to Scott that Americans march on Mexico City and capture the outlying bases, then wait for the Mexican Congress to accept peace terms. Scott, in time seeing that negotiations were getting nowhere, took his enemy's advice: he moved against Mexico City. Now the unbelievable Santa Anna about-faced again. He tried frantically to organize a new army to defend the city! But he bungled, and Scott took the capital.

Santa Anna resigned the presidency and tried to get out of Mexico again. He barely escaped capture by Colonel Jack Hays and a body of 350 Texas Rangers. These stalwarts had gotten General Scott's permission to hunt down the ex-president. In making his getaway Santa Anna probably saved his own life, so bitterly did the Rangers recall Santa Anna's atrocities at the Alamo and Goliad almost 12 years before!

"The Immortal Three-Fourths", as Mexicans now derisively labelled Santa Anna because of his peg leg, had sped away from the Rangers so precipitately that he left behind much of his finery. One of his coats, so heavy with gold braid the Texans felt impelled to weigh it, tipped the scales at 15 pounds. Another jacket, lavishly laden with silver, later provided enough metal for a set of spoons! In future years Santa Anna was to write in his memoirs, "Vanity and glory have never moved me."

"HIS MOST SERENE HIGHNESS"

SANTA ANNA returned to exile. But by 1853 he was back in Mexico. Not only that, he regained the presidency and had himself appointed absolute dictator for one year! He graciously accepted the title of "His Most Serene Highness"! The man had charisma. Once more, however, power turned his head. He grew tyrannical, favored the privileged classes and misappropriated public funds. He was bounced out of Mexico again.

In 1866, while exiled on St. Thomas in the Caribbean, he made his second trip to the U.S. Santa Anna wanted American aid to stamp out the Maximillian-Juarez friction in Mexico — no doubt envisioning himself reinstated as Mexican boss! The U.S. wouldn't help. But he helped the U.S. start a peculiarly American habit: gum chewing! It happened this way. Santa Anna took with him to New York a tropical vegetable called chicle. He liked to cut off chunks of the stuff to chew on. An enterprising young fellow named Bill Adams got hold of some of the chicle and experimented with it. Result: the Adams Chewing Gum Company was founded!

FINAL SCORE

IN THE UNITED STATES Santa Anna is thought of as the villain of the Alamo. And so he was. But while he is not revered in America, he came to be actually hated in Mexico, even during his lifetime. To this day his memory is odious south of the border. Mexicans have always delighted in rearing monuments to even minor personages. But in all Mexico there is not a single statue of Santa Anna. This despite the fact that while in power the Mexican strong man strewed the country with statues of himself.

In considering the attitude of the Mexican people during the Texas Revolution, it ought to be remembered that there were Mexicans who fought on the Texas side. Two of

Santa Anna's earliest opponents were Erasmo Seguin and his son Juan, of San Antonio. Juan Seguin was one of the staunchest fighters for Texas freedom. Three Mexicans signed the Texas Declaration of Independence. Among them was the aristocratic Lorenzo de Zavala who had held high office in Santa Anna's government. But he joined the Texans when it became clear that Santa Anna had made

SANTA ANNA

himself a dictator. Zavala was the first vice president of the Texas Republic.

Perhaps the most damning criticism of Santa Anna is that Karl Marx admired him! In 1861 Marx accused the Spaniards of being degenerate but he praised the ex-dictator of Mexico, stating the "Spanish have never produced a genius the like of Santa Anna."

In February, 1874 Santa Anna, 80 years old, poverty-striken, senile, sick and nearly blind, was permitted to return to Mexico. His compulsion to harangue the populace remained strong. In pity, his young wife Dolores handed pennies to beggars to listen to him and pretend to cheer. He died virtually unnoticed in Mexico City, scene of so many of his triumphs, on June 21, 1876.

6\19

The Cardinal Press
Post Office Box 8288, Dallas, Texas 75205
Printed in the United States of America